Hearing HIM

JOURNAL EDITION

I0804953

© 2021 Cedar Fort, Inc.
All rights reserved.

No part of this book may be reproduced in any form whatsoever, whether by graphic, visual, electronic, film, microfilm, tape recording, or any other means, without prior written permission of the publisher, except in the case of brief passages embodied in critical reviews and articles.

This is not an official publication of The Church of Jesus Christ of Latter-day Saints. The opinions and views expressed herein belong solely to the author and do not necessarily represent the opinions or views of Cedar Fort, Inc. Permission for the use of sources, graphics, and photos is also solely the responsibility of the author.

ISBN 13: 978-1-4621-4050-3

Published by CFI, an imprint of Cedar Fort, Inc.
2373 W. 700 S., Springville, UT, 84663
Distributed by Cedar Fort, Inc., www.cedarfort.com

Cover and interior design by Courtney Proby
Cover design © 2021 Cedar Fort, Inc.

Printed in the United States of America

10 9 8 7 6 5 4 3 2 1

Printed on acid-free paper

Hearing HIM

JOURNAL EDITION

JAMES D. HOLT

CFI
AN IMPRINT OF CEDAR FORT, INC.
SPRINGVILLE, UTAH

Introduction

Behold, the days come, saith the Lord God, that I will send a famine in the land, not a famine of bread, nor a thirst for water, but of hearing the words of the Lord: And they shall wander from sea to sea, and from the north even to the east, they shall run to and fro to seek the word of the Lord, and shall not find it (Amos 8:11–12).

The Prophet Amos foretells of our time when there is a famine of hearing the words of the Lord. As I read this scripture, it seems that it is not for want of trying. Indeed the people that Amos talks about seem to be trying very hard. They are running to and fro but don't seem to be able to hear it. Although it is tempting to limit the people that Amos is talking about to those not on the covenant path, I think Amos could be talking about each of us since circumstances in our lives can make it impossible for us to hear and recognize the voice of the Lord.

The lessons of the scriptures for each of us seems to be that the Lord hasn't stopped speaking to us; it's that we are not hearing Him. This isn't a condemnation of us, and we will explore the various reasons that we can't hear Him later in this book, but what is important is that we recognize that we're not hearing as well as we can and make the changes necessary to ensure that we do. This lesson is taught in the Savior's visitation to the Nephites. In these events, the Nephites gather at the temple and hear a voice they do not understand. They know it is there, but they do not hear it. This happened a second time:

> *And it came to pass that again they heard the voice, and they understood it not. And again the third time they did hear the voice, and did open their ears to hear it; and their eyes were towards the sound thereof; and they did look steadfastly towards heaven, from whence the sound came. And behold, the third time they did understand the voice which they heard . . .* (3 Nephi 11:4–6).

They heard and understood the voice the third time because they opened their ears, turned their eyes toward it, and looked steadfastly to see where it was coming from. In this book we look at ways we can do all of these things in our everyday lives to better hear Him in this time of famine. We will explore this alongside other important questions:

Why is it important to hear Him?

What stops us from trying to hear Him and how can we overcome this to effectively tune in to His messages for us?

Why is it important to hear Him?

God wants us to be like Him. We mature, and with effort we become more like God. We think more of His thoughts and feel more of His feelings. We are one with Him, and our impressions ought to be indistinguishable from His promptings. That unity is one of the things the Savior prayed for. By striving to live as one with Him, you will be more like God and you will "hear Him" and trust Him, even as you trust your own feelings when praying to Him (Jeffrey R. Holland, "To 'Hear Him' Is the Essence of the Restoration").

As I prepare for general conference, why is it important for me to hear Him now?

What are the questions I have that I hope to have answered as I try to hear Him?

When we speak of Hearing Him (whether the Father, Son, or Holy Ghost), it is usually through the Holy Ghost that we are able to hear. We know through the unity of the Godhead that what one speaks is as what all would speak. The way we usually hear the Father or the Son is through the ministration of the Holy Ghost. Before we receive the Gift of the Holy Ghost, we are able to receive inspiration from the light—or Spirit—of Christ and visitations of the Holy Ghost. It is after baptism and confirmation that we are able to have the constant companionship of the Holy Ghost. Whatever stage of the path we are on, the command to "'hear Him" follows the same pattern but comes in many different ways. The Prophet Joel foretold:

Your sons and your daughters shall prophesy, your old men shall dream dreams, your young men shall see visions: and also upon the servants and upon the handmaids in those days will I pour out my spirit (Joel 2:28–29).

The modes of revelation or Hearing Him in this verse are dreams and visions. These are only two of many ways the Holy Ghost can communicate with us. In my life, I have felt the promptings of the Holy Ghost in many different ways, and these promptings are part of the admonition of the scriptures:

And he humbled thee, and suffered thee to hunger, and fed thee with manna, which thou knewest not, neither did thy fathers know; that he might make thee know that man doth not live by bread only, but by every word that proceedeth out of the mouth of the Lord doth man live (Deuteronomy 8:3).

While it is tempting to apply the above scripture and others like it to scriptures or the words of modern-day prophets and apostles, we need to recognize that personal revelation—the promptings of the Holy Ghost—are words that proceed forth out of the mouth of the Lord. We cannot live successfully or hope for eternal life without the promptings of the Holy Ghost. The Holy Ghost is the means by which we Hear in our minds the will of the Godhead. It is our responsibility to live in a way that enables us to hear the Holy Ghost in our lives, and this means drawing close to Him. To do this, we have to understand the importance of the Holy Ghost in Hearing Him.

At the end of a PhD in the UK, the student has what is called a "viva." This is where carefully chosen people in your field examine your work for a couple of hours and ask you questions. The purpose of this is to ensure your work has a high enough standard and that it is your own work. During my viva I got into an interesting discussion about the nature of God. I had disagreed with something my examiner had written about Latter-day Saints only worshiping the Father and the Son. The Holy Ghost was somewhat of an afterthought in his opinion. His argument was that we did not speak about the Holy Ghost enough. Although I disagreed, it caused me to stop and wonder how he would have arrived at such a position. I was, and still am, very careful to talk about the roles of the Holy Ghost so that no one can make that observation again. As we explore the roles of the Holy Ghost, we realize why it is so important to hear Him every day of our lives. The roles of the Holy Ghost include

Revelation
Testifying of the Father and the Son
Guidance
Comfort
Sealing
Sanctification
Gifts of the Spirit
Effect a change of heart

Never did any passage of scripture come with more power to the heart of man than this did at this time to mine. It seemed to enter with great force into every feeling of my heart. I reflected on it again and again...

(JSH 1:12).

Finding comfort through hearing Him

Throughout my life, and with varying degrees of regularity, I have received these blessings from the Holy Ghost. I remember my very first spiritual experience that helped me understand the peace that can come to our lives. I was 8 years old and on a school exchange to France. I was staying with a family that I did not know. I remember going to bed in an attic of a home where I barely understood anybody. This was my first time away from home, and I was crying because I missed home so much. My mum had taught me the importance of prayer, and although my feelings of homesickness seemed to drown everything else out, I decided I should kneel by the side of my bed and pray. While praying, I felt a comfort to my heart to know that someone was looking after me and all would be well. This formative experience has served me well through the years as I have found myself in similar situations that seemed to be overwhelming—whether the outcome was a lack of self-worth or a feeling of hopelessness when faced with the illnesses of loved ones. I knew I could reach out and hear Him through the Holy Ghost and feel the loving arms of the Savior around me. That same blessing is available for each of us if we take time to reach out and hear Him.

I can't imagine my life without the comfort of the Holy Ghost. We can experience each of these roles/gifts of the Holy Ghost in our daily lives. It is important that Hearing Him is a daily experience. We are, to use the analogy given by the Savior in the story of the wise and foolish virgins (Matthew 25:1–13), putting oil into our lamps on a daily basis, and the Holy Ghost is integral to the process.

As we look at each of the roles above, we can perhaps think of circumstances when each one becomes important to recognize.

Undoubtedly with some sadness, the Master over every problem and fear, He who is the solution to every discouragement and disappointment, stretched out His hand and grasped the drowning disciple with the gentle rebuke, "O thou of little faith, wherefore didst thou doubt?"

If you are lonely, please know you can find comfort. If you are discouraged, please know you can find hope. If you are poor in spirit, please know you can be strengthened. If you feel you are broken, please know you can be mended (Jeffrey R. Holland, "Broken Things to Mend").

When have I felt comfort through the Holy Ghost and the Atonement of Jesus Christ?

Finding sanctification through hearing Him

In the Book of Mormon, we read of various individuals who received sanctification to their souls, or forgiveness of their sins. One of my favorites is Enos, who in quite a matter of fact way describes his experience:

> *And my soul hungered; and I kneeled down before my Maker, and I cried unto him in mighty prayer and supplication for mine own soul; and all the day long did I cry unto him; yea, and when the night came I did still raise my voice high that it reached the heavens. And there came a voice unto me, saying: Enos, thy sins are forgiven thee, and thou shalt be blessed. And I, Enos, knew that God could not lie; wherefore, my guilt was swept away. And I said: Lord, how is it done? And he said unto me: Because of thy faith in Christ, whom thou hast never before heard nor seen. And many years pass away before he shall manifest himself in the flesh; wherefore, go to, thy faith hath made thee whole (Enos 1:4–8).*

Enos' experience of hearing the voice of the Lord through the Holy Ghost confirms the forgiveness of sins and his sanctification. Through his humility, yearning, and reliance on the Lord, his guilt is swept away. This enables him to labor with all diligence for the people of Nephi. A similar experience can be found in the life of Alma the Younger. He is much more descriptive about his process of repentance and sanctification:

And now, behold, when I thought this, I could remember my pains no more; yea, I was harrowed up by the memory of my sins no more. And oh, what joy, and what marvelous light I did behold; yea, my soul was filled with joy as exceeding as was my pain! Yea, I say unto you, my son, that there could be nothing so exquisite and so bitter as were my pains. Yea, and again I say unto you, my son, that on the other hand, there can be nothing so exquisite and sweet as was my joy (Alma 36:19–21).

Again, it motivated Alma to serve others and live continually in a relationship with the Lord. Sometimes we can look at these experiences and be overawed them. Although I am certainly a sinner, I don't think I measure up to the description that Alma gives of his sins, so maybe the turnaround in my life is not as sudden or as stark. We should not expect such a dramatic experience. Nevertheless, the assurance that I have been forgiven and can stand in the Lord's presence in the future is just as important tomorrow as it was yesterday and is today. It may not come through an angel, but knowing that angels speak by the power of the Holy Ghost, we are able to immediately receive the assurance of the Holy Ghost directly. When I partake of the sacrament each week I can receive the sanctification of my soul by the Holy Ghost (through the Atonement of Jesus Christ) to ensure I can continue in my relationship with the Lord.

I have served as a bishop for over eleven years, and during that time, different individuals have come to me as a representative so they can activate the sanctifying power of the Atonement and the Holy Ghost in their lives. Sometimes this has meant that they have had to stop partaking of the sacrament for a period of time. It is through our discussions and the removal of this blessing that many have come to realize the importance of the sacrament on a weekly basis. It really does rejuvenate and inspire us to do and be better.

The sacrament is necessary to obtain access to the power of godliness. That we might more fully keep ourselves unspotted from the world, we are commanded to go to the house of prayer and offer up our sacraments upon the Lord's holy day. Please consider that the emblems of the Lord's body and blood, the bread and the water, are both blessed and sanctified. "O God, the Eternal Father, we ask thee in the name of thy Son, Jesus Christ, to bless and sanctify this bread [or this water] to the souls of all those who partake [or drink] of it." To sanctify is to make pure and holy. The sacramental emblems are sanctified in remembrance of Christ's purity, of our total dependence upon His Atonement, and of our responsibility to so honor our ordinances and covenants that we can "stand spotless before [Him] at the last day."

The ordinance of the sacrament is a holy and repeated invitation to repent sincerely and to be renewed spiritually. The act of partaking of the sacrament, in and of itself, does not remit sins. But as we prepare conscientiously and participate in this holy ordinance with a broken heart and a contrite spirit, then the promise is that we may always have the Spirit of the Lord to be with us. And by the sanctifying power of the Holy Ghost as our constant companion, we can always retain a remission of our sins. We truly are blessed each week by the opportunity to evaluate our lives through the ordinance of the sacrament, to renew our covenants, and to receive this covenant promise (David A. Bednar, "Always Retain a Remission of Your Sins").

As I prepare to take the sacrament, what are the things I need to place on the altar before the Lord and be sanctified through the Holy Ghost and the Atonement of Jesus Christ?

Becoming a new creature through hearing Him

The reception of the Holy Ghost and process of sanctification makes us a new creature in Christ. It is not a passive relationship. Our indwelling with the Holy Ghost and the activation of the Atonement entails the removal of sin and its replacement with Christlike qualities. Parley P. Pratt has described that the Holy Ghost actively

> *. . . quickens all the intellectual faculties, increases, enlarges, expands, and purifies all the natural passions and affections, and adapts them, by the gift of wisdom, to their lawful use. [He] inspires, develops, cultivates, and matures all the fine-toned sympathies, joys, tastes, kindred feelings, and affections of our nature. [He] inspires virtue, kindness, goodness, tenderness, gentleness, and charity. [He] develops beauty of person, form, and features. [He] tends to health, vigor, animation, and social feeling. [He] invigorates all the faculties of the physical and intellectual man. [He] strengthens and gives tone to the nerves. In short, [he] is, as it were, marrow to the bone, joy to the heart, light to the eyes, music to the ears, and life to the whole being*
> *(Parley P. Pratt,* Key to the Science of Theology*, 61).*

Listen...

This change of heart is, however, not a one-time event. It is something that we have to recapture every day of our lives through Hearing Him. In our daily interactions with the Godhead, we are able to develop more of their characteristics and qualities. It is by spending time Hearing Him that we are able to become more like them, to become more Christlike. We can see evidence of this in our daily interactions with others. As I think about this, I think about people throughout my life who have changed aspects of my behavior or character. Most obviously is my wife. When I first met Ruth, I was about to turn 20, and having just returned home from my mission, I had the fashion sense of a 17-year-old. I had Garfield T-shirts, Bermuda shorts, and other disturbing items in my wardrobe. Over a few months, and with certain gifts from Ruth, my wardrobe changed. I no longer wore—and still don't wear today—comic book T-shirts. Ruth has also changed me in many other ways in the nearly thirty years we have been together. Her kind heart and compassion have made me much more aware of how I treat other people and the impact my words can have on others. I often consider how Ruth would respond, and that has become second nature to me so that I am kinder.

If we allow a relationship to end, those influences can fade over time. We're often told that we receive "line upon line." Sometimes that works in reverse so that even what we have "shall be taken away" (2 Nephi 28:30). We cannot live on past revelation, relationships, and spiritual experiences forever. We need to receive revelations every day throughout our lives (Helaman 11:23). Living the gospel is like walking up an escalator the wrong way. We cannot stay in the same place. As my eldest daughter, Eleanor, served her mission, she asked why she had not heard many of the spiritual experiences I had on my mission (though she had heard the funny ones). As I thought about this, I realized that it wasn't because I hadn't had any. It was quite the opposite. It was that those experiences have been replaced in my immediate memory by new ones. I wasn't relying on my mission experiences to remember what the Spirit felt like. I was/am daily receiving revelation upon revelation.

You may ask, "Why doesn't this mighty change happen more quickly with me?" You should remember that the remarkable examples of King Benjamin's people, Alma, and some others in scripture are just that—remarkable and not typical. For most of us, the changes are more gradual and occur over time. Being born again, unlike our physical birth, is more a process than an event. And engaging in that process is the central purpose of mortality (D. Todd Christofferson, "Born Again").

As I look back on my life, what things have changed that show my desire to be a disciple of Jesus Christ?

Receiving revelation through hearing Him

Because our Heavenly Father wants better for us, He makes it possible for us to hear His voice. Most often, we hear Him through impressions given by the Holy Ghost. The Holy Ghost is the third member of the Godhead. He witnesses of the Father and the Son, was sent to "teach [us] all things," and will "show unto [us] all things what [we] should do."

The Spirit speaks to different people in different ways, and He may speak to the same person in different ways at different times. As a result, learning the many ways He speaks to us is a lifelong quest. Sometimes, He speaks to our "mind and in [our] heart" in a voice that is small yet powerful, piercing "them that . . . hear to the center." Other times His impressions "occupy [our] mind[s]" or "press . . . upon [our] feelings." Other times our bosom will "burn within [us]." Still other times He fills our souls with joy, enlightens our minds, or speaks peace to our troubled hearts. We will find our Father's voice in many places (David P. Homer, "Hearing His Voice").

Revelation through the Holy Ghost is to know the mind and will of the Lord. In our daily lives, it is to know of His will for each of us as individuals. He knows us better than we know ourselves. It is such a blessing to know of the truthfulness of things and to receive guidance as to what we should do and how we should live. Revelation and guidance from the Holy Ghost are thus crucial to the successful living of life:

Nephi taught this: "If ye will . . . receive the Holy Ghost, it will show unto you all things what ye should do" (2 Ne. 32:5). What a remarkable privilege and promise! Lorenzo Snow said that it is the "grand privilege of every Latter-day Saint . . . to have the manifestations of the Spirit every day of our lives . . . [so] that we may know the light, and not be groveling continually in the dark." And his sister Eliza R. Snow declared: "You may talk to the [Saints] about the follies of the world... till dooms day, and it will make no impression. But . . . place them in a position where they will get the Holy Ghost, and that will be a sure protection against outside influences." We have been promised the constant companionship of the third member of the Godhead and hence the privilege of receiving revelation for our own lives. We are not alone!
(Sheri L. Dew, We Are Not Alone, *94).*

The process of revelation gives us surety and power. We are able to go forward with faith and confidence in our choices as they are grounded in the Lord Jesus Christ. The process of revelation is described by the Lord in the Doctrine and Covenants:

Yea, behold, I will tell you in your mind and in your heart, by the Holy Ghost, which shall come upon you and which shall dwell in your heart (D&C 8:2–3).

The use of our minds and hearts in the communication of the Holy Ghost is emphasized in the early searching of Joseph Smith after reading James 1:5. He describes the revelation of the Holy Ghost perfectly:

Never did any passage of scripture come with more power to the heart of man than this did at this time to mine. It seemed to enter with great force into every feeling of my heart. I reflected on it again and again (JSH 1:12).

It came to him in his mind and heart. This is the same process and revelation that we can go through. It feels right in our hearts and makes sense in our minds. While we often talk about the promptings of the Holy Ghost, sometimes we don't understand the power of the Holy Ghost and the strength it can provide to each of us, especially as we receive revelation through Him from the Lord. The Doctrine and Covenants continues:

> *Now, behold, this is the spirit of revelation; behold, this is the spirit by which Moses brought the children of Israel through the Red Sea on dry ground. Therefore this is thy gift; apply unto it, and blessed art thou, for it shall deliver you out of the hands of your enemies, when, if it were not so, they would slay you and bring your soul to destruction (D&C 8:2–3).*

This spirit of revelation enabled Moses to part the Red Sea, and it has the power to deliver us out of the hands of our enemies. When we think of enemies, we can consider not just Satan but also the associated feelings and problems we face in this world, whatever they may be. Most people are familiar with the poem "Footprints," which I think this is appropriate here. The Savior's Atonement and the Holy Ghost work together to carry us through every aspect of our lives. We are strengthened, comforted, and guided every step of the way. Revelation helps us not only know what to do. It can also reveal to us who we are and our standing before the Lord. As I think about my life, one of the things I have had to struggle with is the "impostor syndrome." This wasn't something I knew had a name until a couple of years ago. I thought I was the only one who struggled with it. It is a thought process within me that convinces me I am a fraud; that everything I claim to be and do is only a mask that I'm fooling people with. I was sure that at some point someone would discover this deception and unmask me. Although now and again I still suffer from it, I have realized that through my relationship with deity that I am of divine heritage. I have been put on this earth to succeed. This is just one example, but knowing that Hearing the Lord and His voice can help us overcome the constant barrage of doubt, challenges, and criticism we face is of immeasurable value.

One of the most important things we can do is to become familiar with the promptings of the Holy Ghost and how to hear Him. I consider myself as having joined the Church as a teenager. I was baptized when I was 8 but didn't attend meetings until I was 15. When I started coming to Church and for a couple of years afterward, I felt I had a problem with my testimony and my relationship with God. I knew the Holy Ghost came into your mind and heart. For the longest time I only seemed to understand things in my mind. Some things felt right, but I didn't think I had experienced any of the things of the heart that are promised as part of the process of revelation. What made it worse is the description in Doctrine and Covenants 9 where the Holy Ghost is a burning in the bosom. I knew I had definitely not experienced that. This was a real obstacle for me. I didn't question the gospel and its truths. Rather, I questioned my spirituality and self-worth. Was I not worth communicating with?

I was blessed with some amazing teachers and leaders who helped me through this stage of doubt—again not doubting the Lord, but doubting myself. They helped me recognize when I was feeling the Holy Ghost in my life. I distinctly remember one occasion where a teacher said, "Jimmy, how you are feeling right now? That is the Holy Ghost." He was right. He knew because he also felt it. This was a moment of revelation; a light bulb moment when the scales fell from my eyes. I realized that the scriptures spoke in metaphors when describing the feelings of the Holy Ghost. I had felt the Holy Ghost many times throughout my life. I just didn't recognize it until it was pointed out to me. I was then able to look back over various experiences and come to know how blessed I had been.

Trying to describe the feelings of the Holy Ghost in a specific way is difficult. The philosopher William James used the word "ineffable" when he described religious experiences. Ineffable means that something is impossible to put into words. For me, on different occasions the Holy Ghost has felt like a nervous excitement, a peace, or a confidence in the course I have set. I don't know how the Holy Ghost feels for you. I do know that those feelings involve the heart and the mind, but the specific feelings you need to describe for yourself or to help those close to you to understand how the Holy Ghost works in your life can only come from you.

This power associated with Hearing His voice and focusing on Him is shown in the story of Peter walking on the water. The story begins with Jesus walking on the water and the disciples seeing Him.

But straightway Jesus spake unto them, saying, Be of good cheer; it is I; be not afraid. And Peter answered him and said, Lord, if it be thou, bid me come unto thee on the water. And he said, Come. And when Peter was come down out of the ship, he walked on the water, to go to Jesus. But when he saw the wind boisterous, he was afraid; and beginning to sink, he cried, saying, Lord, save me. And immediately Jesus stretched forth his hand, and caught him, and said unto him, O thou of little faith, wherefore didst thou doubt?
(Matthew 14:27–31).

Peter initially heard the voice of the Lord and responded. In doing so, he was able to walk on the water. It was only when he took his focus off the Savior and worried about all the other things that swirled around him that he began to sink. At least he was able to recognize he was sinking and shout to the Lord for help. This is the perfect parallel for our attempts to Hear the Lord and stay in a relationship with Him where we feel such confidence and power. We begin with the surety that we have heard the Lord, but other competing voices come into our minds, and we begin to lose confidence in what we thought we heard. Perhaps we then wander into strange paths rather than sink. We are distracted from the necessity of and the strength that comes from Hearing Him on a daily basis. This will be explored further in the next section of this book.

As indicated by the list of the roles of the Holy Ghost, there are many other aspects that could highlight the importance of Hearing Him in our lives, but I have used just a few examples to illustrate the absolute necessity of Hearing Him each day.

Think of your own life. Over the years I have listened to thousands of profoundly spiritual experiences from Latter-day Saints all across the world, confirming to me beyond any question that God knows and loves each of us and that He eagerly desires to reveal Himself to us. These experiences may come at pivotal times in our lives or in what may at first seem as uneventful happenings, but they are always accompanied by an exceptionally strong spiritual confirmation of the love of God.

Remembering these spiritually defining experiences sends us to our knees, declaring as did the Prophet Joseph, "What I received was from heaven. I know it, and I know that God knows that I know it" (Neil L. Andersen, "Spiritually Defining Memories").

What revelations have I received in my life?
How often am I asking for and receiving revelation?

"ineffable"
WILLIAM JAMES

What stops us from trying to hear Him?

How can we overcome this to effectively
tune in to His messages for us?

In the last section, we looked briefly at the story of Peter walking on water. Hearing the voice of the Lord gave him the strength and power to overcome his fears and all of the other things that sought to bring him down. It was only when he lost focus and paid attention to the things around him that he began to sink. We sometimes find ourselves in Peter's position. We want to hear Him but there are so many other things that vie for our attention. Why we find this so hard is hinted at in the scriptures:

And he said, Go forth, and stand upon the mount before the Lord. And, behold, the Lord passed by, and a great and strong wind rent the mountains, and brake in pieces the rocks before the Lord; but the Lord was not in the wind: and after the wind an earthquake; but the Lord was not in the earthquake: And after the earthquake a fire; but the Lord was not in the fire: and after the fire a still small voice (1 Kings 19:11–12).

And it came to pass when they heard this voice, and beheld that it was not a voice of thunder, neither was it a voice of a great tumultuous noise, but behold, it was a still voice of perfect mildness, as if it had been a whisper, and it did pierce even to the very soul . . . (Helaman 5:30)

We live in a noisy world. The voice of the Lord is not noisy and does not engage in shouting matches. It is a still small voice that can often be drowned out by other seemingly urgent and distracting voices if we allow it to be. When we are learning to hear the voice of the Holy Ghost, the analogy of trying to tune in a radio station is often used. James E. Faust once shared this:

My first radio was a crystal set. It was hard to tune to the frequency of a particular radio station. One had to literally scratch the receiving wire whisker over the top of the rough crystal to find the right pinpoint, a little valley or peak on the crystal, where the signal was received. Just a millimeter off on one side or the other of that point and you would lose the signal and get scratchy static. Over time, with patience and perseverance, good eyesight and a steady hand, you could learn to find the signal point on the crystal without too much difficulty.

So it is in learning to attune ourselves to the inspiration from God and tune out the scratchy static. We have to work at being tuned in. Most of us need a long time to become tuned in most of the time. When I was a young General Authority, President Marion G. Romney, who was in his seventies at the time, told us, "I know when I am working under the Spirit and when I am not." To be able to recognize when one is being guided by the Spirit is a supernal gift
(Stories From My Life, *49*).

When I first heard this analogy, it was dated. I don't know what a crystal set is, but I am old enough to remember being in the back garden listening to the cricket on a radio and spending the first ten minutes turning the dial on the radio to ensure that the reception was just right and that I could hear clearly. As I think about my children, maybe this analogy is even more dated. The radio we listen to in the car is preset. We just press a button and the station is found and the music is clear. What is there today that has the same kind of precision tuning? Maybe it's the search for a phone signal. Recently my eldest daughter went on a hike up Mount Snowden in North Wales. For the seven-hour hike, Eleanor's phone was out of signal range. When her group reached a restaurant, she realized she had a number of messages from her parents checking if she was okay. Thus began a trek up the road, searching for the sweet spot that would give her a mobile signal. I think we've all been there.

Whatever analogy we use it is important to recognize that it takes effort to find the right environment for us to feel the Holy Ghost and to hear Him. The frequency doesn't change, but our ability to hear it does. The Book of Mormon teaches us this principle in a way that is very important. King Benjamin tells us that "ye do withdraw yourselves from the Spirit of the Lord, that it may have no place in you to guide you in wisdom's paths that ye may be blessed, prospered, and preserved" (Mosiah 2:36). It is not the Holy Ghost that moves, it is us. That means that as we explore the various ways that stop us from Hearing Him, it is important to recognize that we have the ability to overcome all of the things that might be hindering us from hearing the voice of the Lord.

What are some of the voices that interfere with our ability to hear Him?

Some of the voices that can distract us from Hearing Him are external, and some are internal that come from within ourselves. The words of the Psalmist to "Be still, and know that I am God" (Psalm 46:10) will be explored in greater detail later, but for now I would like to highlight that the noisiness and busyness of life can sometimes mean that we can't take time to be still. We're always faced with noise or other things vying for our attention.

We live in a world with many voices seeking our attention. With all the breaking news, tweets, blogs, podcasts, and compelling advice from Alexa, Siri, and others, we can find it difficult to know which voices to trust. Sometimes we crowd source guidance in our lives, thinking the majority will provide the best source of truth. Other times we "halt . . . between two opinions," choosing to be "neither cold nor hot." Still other times we follow what is convenient, focus on a single voice or issue to guide us, or rely exclusively upon our own ability to think. While each of these approaches can be helpful, experience teaches that they are not always reliable. What is popular is not always what is best. Halting between two opinions brings no direction. Convenience rarely leads to things that matter. Fixation on a single voice or issue can impair our ability to see. And relying solely upon our own thinking can lead us into a hyperintellectual stupor of thought. If we are not careful, the wrong voices can draw us away from the gospel center to places where faith is difficult to sustain, and we find little more than emptiness, bitterness, and dissatisfaction (David P. Homer, "Hearing His Voice").

What are some of the voices that interfere
with my ability to hear Him?

The busyness of life

Life is busy. As a teenager we may face an overload of schoolwork. We may also face a social calendar that is filled with worthwhile activities to develop and nurture friendships. We might have part-time work. We have Church responsibilities, after-school clubs, hobbies, and all kinds of other things. As an adult we are similarly faced with family activities, Church service, work, activities, friends, hobbies, and much more. None of these are wrong, and all of them are important, but sometimes we get caught up in being so busy that we sometimes don't take time to pause and listen to the voice of the Lord. We can perhaps think that He is not speaking or that we are functioning just fine as we travel through life. Speaking of the untimely death of a son of a member of the Presiding Bishopric, President David O. McKay shared the following about a visitation of the son to his mother:

"Mother, you needn't worry. That was merely an accident. I gave the signal to the engineer to move on, and as the train started, I jumped for the handle of the freight car, and my foot got caught in a sagebrush, and I fell under the wheel. I went to father soon after that, but he was so busy in the office I couldn't influence him—I couldn't make any impression upon him, and I tried again. Today I come to you to give you that comfort and tell you that I am happy" (David O. McKay, Gospel Ideals, *525–26).*

This highlights the very real possibility that we allow ourselves to get so busy that we don't have time to listen. The voices of busyness are not bad in themselves, but they are loud, and if we allow them to, they can drown out the still small voice.

There are also times when these voices of busyness taking precedence in our lives are the result of our deliberate choices to ignore the voice of the Lord. We have prioritized our work or recreation over the still small voice, and perhaps we have justified this to ourselves that this is what is needed. The voices that entice us with the need to have more money so that we can afford certain items, or working for the next promotion because that will make life easier, or the hobby that enables us to unwind a little bit. None of these are wrong in and of themselves, except when we prioritize them above our relationship with the Savior and our ability to hear Him. In some ways it is trusting Him that He will fulfill the promises that he has made that if we "seek ye first the kingdom of God and his righteousness . . . all these things shall be added unto you" (3 Nephi 13:33).

This is both more difficult and easier than it sounds. Shortly after joining the Church, I read a quote from Joseph Fielding Smith that troubled me. He said:

> *Who should we love above everything else in the world? . . . The Lord and Savior Jesus Christ. Love him more than we do our own lives, or our own fathers and mothers or children; . . . because without his blessings we would have nothing (*Take Heed to Yourselves, *296).*

How is this possible? Surely it is impossible to love anybody more than we love our spouse and children. I remember pondering on the quote and praying that I could have an understanding of such guidance. I then heard wonderful instruction, that as we love the Savior, our capacity to love other people grows so much more. Loving Jesus first enables me to have a deeper and more abiding love for all the people around me. At a very basic level, I am able to love my family longer (for eternity) as I place the Savior in the forefront of my life. However, the quality and expression of my love becomes so much more sincere and deeper as I focus on the Savior. This love is not just limited to our families. Our ability to love others and show that love is enhanced.

If we seek the Lord first in our lives, then all of our activities will be strengthened because we are Hearing Him first, so we will always know of His will and guidance in our lives. This is about focusing on our spirituality and not necessarily how busy we are. Whenever I extend a calling to an individual, I generally share with them the story behind section 10 of the Doctrine and Covenants. At this point, Joseph Smith is not long married, has a farm to keep, and after only just having received permission to resume translating again, the preparation of the Book of Mormon is paramount. Despite all of this, the Lord gives him the following warning:

> *Do not run faster or labor more than you have strength and means provided to enable you to translate; but be diligent unto the end (D&C 10:4).*

Yes, the work with which Joseph was entrusted was important, but he was not to try to do it all at once. Even though he was encouraged to be sensible with his time, in the next verse there is something that Joseph is told not to neglect:

> *Pray always, that you may come off conqueror; yea, that you may conquer Satan, and that you may escape the hands of the servants of Satan that do uphold his work (D&C 10:5).*

With all of the plates that Joseph had spinning, the "thing" that enabled him to keep them spinning was the Spirit he received through his personal worship. To that we can add prayer, scripture study, partaking of the sacrament, attending the Temple, and more. In short, all of these things enable us to have the Holy Ghost more in our lives.

There have been times in my life when I was not great at this, but if I look over the last thirty or so years of my Church membership, I can see the blessings that have come into my life because of me always seeking to put the Savior first. Probably one of the earliest examples is with my studies. From the age of 15 onward, I have always been conscientious in studying the scriptures, as well as in keeping up with my school and university work. While there were huge pressure points at certain times, such as when I was completing formal exams at the ages of 16 and 18, my scripture study and daily prayers were non-negotiable. I can't say that studying my scriptures changed my grades, but they certainly gave me the perspective and grounding I needed for my wider studies.

I love the Old Testament story of a young man who served the prophet Elisha. Early one morning, the young man woke up, went outside, and found the city surrounded by a great army intent on destroying them. He ran to Elisha: "Alas, my master! how shall we do?" Elisha answered, "Fear not: for they that be with us are more than they that be with them."

Elisha knew the young man needed more than calming reassurance; he needed vision. And so "Elisha prayed, . . . Lord, . . . open his eyes, that he may see. And the Lord opened the eyes of the young man; and he saw: and, behold, the mountain was full of horses and chariots of fire round about Elisha."

> *There may be times when you, like the servant, find yourself struggling to see how God is working in your life—times when you feel under siege—when the trials of mortality bring you to your knees. Wait and trust in God and in His timing, because you can trust His heart with all of yours. But there is a second lesson here. My dear sisters and brothers, you too can pray for the Lord to open your eyes to see things you would not normally see.*
> *(Michelle D. Craig, "Eyes to See").*

What are the things that I have competing for my time?

Is there an appropriate balance in my life?
How can I seek first the kingdom of God?

The voices of opposition

Sometimes the voices that we hear are ones that are in opposition to the principles of the Restored Gospel of Jesus Christ. We are given a formula in the Book of Mormon to help us identify what these voices/temptations are:

. . . whatsoever thing persuadeth men to do evil, and believe not in Christ, and deny him, and serve not God, then ye may know with a perfect knowledge it is of the devil; for after this manner doth the devil work, for he persuadeth no man to do good, no, not one; neither do his angels; neither do they who subject themselves unto him (Moroni 7:17).

Anything that tries to draw us away from the Savior is not of God. Unfortunately, while some choices may be obvious, others are not as Satan tries to "leadeth them away carefully down to hell" (2 Nephi 28:31). The voices are loud, but they are also subtle and flattering. They are voices that try to make good look evil, and evil look good. So many of these voices are vying for our attention. The obvious ones that we can see include pornography, drugs, alcohol, and immorality. The more subtle ones may include those that take us away from the Savior by degrees. It may be a song that encourages immorality, but we don't really listen to the words until we find ourselves singing along to it. Or it may be a film we are watching that makes us hope that one of the characters acts immorally. For each of these, we need to be conscious of what we are letting into our homes, our minds, and our hearts.

MY FAITH IS AN INTEGRAL PART OF WHO I AM.

AS A DISCIPLE OF CHRIST, MY DISCIPLESHIP

SHOULD INFUSE EVERY ASPECT OF MY LIFE.

I STRIVE TO KEEP THE ARMOR OF GOD

MOLDED TO ME.

I VIEW IT MORE AS

WOLVERINE'S ADAMANTIUM

RATHER THAN IRON MAN'S SUIT.

IT IS NOT A BOLT ON AND OFF ACCESSORY.

As we seek to be disciples of Jesus Christ, our efforts to hear Him need to be ever more intentional. It takes conscious and consistent effort to fill our daily lives with His words, His teachings, His truths. We simply cannot rely upon information we bump into on social media. With billions of words online and in a marketing-saturated world constantly infiltrated by noisy, nefarious efforts of the adversary, where can we go to hear Him?
(Russell M. Nelson, "Hear Him")

What are the voices that try to distract me from Hearing Him?

____

____

____

____

____

____

____

How can I more intentionally hear Him?

____

____

____

____

____

____

____

____

____

Two ways to remove the voices of opposition

The scriptures teach us of two ways we can remove these voices from our lives and prevent them from taking root. First, the Savior suggests:

> *And if thy right eye offend thee, pluck it out, and cast it from thee: for it is profitable for thee that one of thy members should perish, and not that thy whole body should be cast into hell. And if thy right hand offend thee, cut it off, and cast it from thee: for it is profitable for thee that one of thy members should perish, and not that thy whole body should be cast into hell (Matthew 5:29–30).*

This all sounds rather extreme, but I think the words the Savior uses are specifically chosen for that purpose. He is highlighting how dangerous such actions are and that we need to immediately remove them from our lives. We make a specific and long-lasting decision that we do not allow such influences into our lives from that moment on.

When I was a teenager, this meant that I had to make decisions about the films I would watch, the people I would date, the music I would listen to, and the standards I would keep. Life as an adult has been much easier (not necessarily easy) because of the decisions I made early on in my gospel living to avoid those actions and tempting voices that would lead me away from the Savior. These voices are individual to each of us. Satan knows us well and how to best distract us from hearing the voice of the Lord. These may be the voices of discouragement, lack of self-worth, the enticement of sin, and many more. Satan personalizes the weapons he uses for each of us. I have a slightly addictive personality which has manifested itself in my adult life in terms of my mobile phone usage. Many people can play games on their phone. I found that if I downloaded a game I would spend all my spare time on it. Fortunately I realized this and deleted the apps from my phone so I wouldn't be tempted again. This is reminiscent (though on a sillier level) of the people of Ammon in the Book of Mormon who "buried their weapons of war" because they feared "to take them up lest by any means they should sin; yea, ye can see that they fear to sin" (Helaman 15:9). We must put our temptations out of reach so we can more effectively hear Him.

In contrast, the distractions and noise that fill the world, our homes, and our lives can make it more difficult to hear His voice. These distractions can so occupy our minds and hearts that we leave no room for the gentle promptings of the Holy Ghost.

The Prophet Joseph Smith taught that most often God reveals Himself "to individuals in private, in their chamber; in the wilderness or fields, and that generally without noise or tumult."

> *Satan wants to separate us from God's voice by keeping us out of those quiet places. If God speaks in a still, small voice, you and I need to draw close to hear Him. Just imagine what would happen if we were as intent on staying connected with heaven as we are on staying connected to Wi-Fi! Pick a time and place, and listen for God's voice every day. And keep this sacred appointment with exactness, for so very much depends on it!*
> *(Michelle D. Craig, "Spiritual Capacity")*

Are there any things in my life that are worrisome distractions?
What can I do to mute them?

The second way that the scriptures teach us to prevent these voices from taking root in our lives is found in the Book of Mormon as the Nephites made their preparations for war. Captain Moroni had his people construct defenses:

> *And he caused that they should build a breastwork of timbers upon the inner bank of the ditch; and they cast up dirt out of the ditch against the breastwork of timbers; and thus they did cause the Lamanites to labor until they had encircled the city of Bountiful round about with a strong wall of timbers and earth, to an exceeding height (Alma 53:4).*

If we wish to restrict the influence of these tempting voices in our lives and homes, we have to create robust defenses. These are similar to the defenses discussed in cutting things off that lead us away from the Savior or have us withdraw ourselves from the Spirit. As we look at our lives and our homes, what are the influences we are allowing in? This doesn't mean that the only things we allow into our homes are Church produced and focused; rather that the things we allow in do not muddy the waters and lead us carefully away. It is interesting to me how the challenges that face young people (and adults) today have developed in such a way that they are hard to avoid. The first time I served as a bishop was prior to the explosion of social media and the easy accessibility of the Internet throughout our homes. (This was in 2000–2004). This time as I serve as bishop, the way I talk about the influences in life has changed. Whereas in the past I might have taught about avoiding pornography, now I teach what to do when we are faced with it. Pornography is now unfiltered in spite of all our efforts to filter it.

The defenses we put into place in our lives and homes are very much focused around the armor of God spoken of in the scriptures. (See Ephesians 6:11–18 and D&C 27:15–18.) Each of these pieces of armor are related to the Holy Ghost and the power we find through Him. We are promised that in donning this armor, living with faith, having a hope of salvation, preparing for each day through study and prayer, keeping ourselves physically, mentally, and spiritually healthy, and following the promptings of the Lord in living a

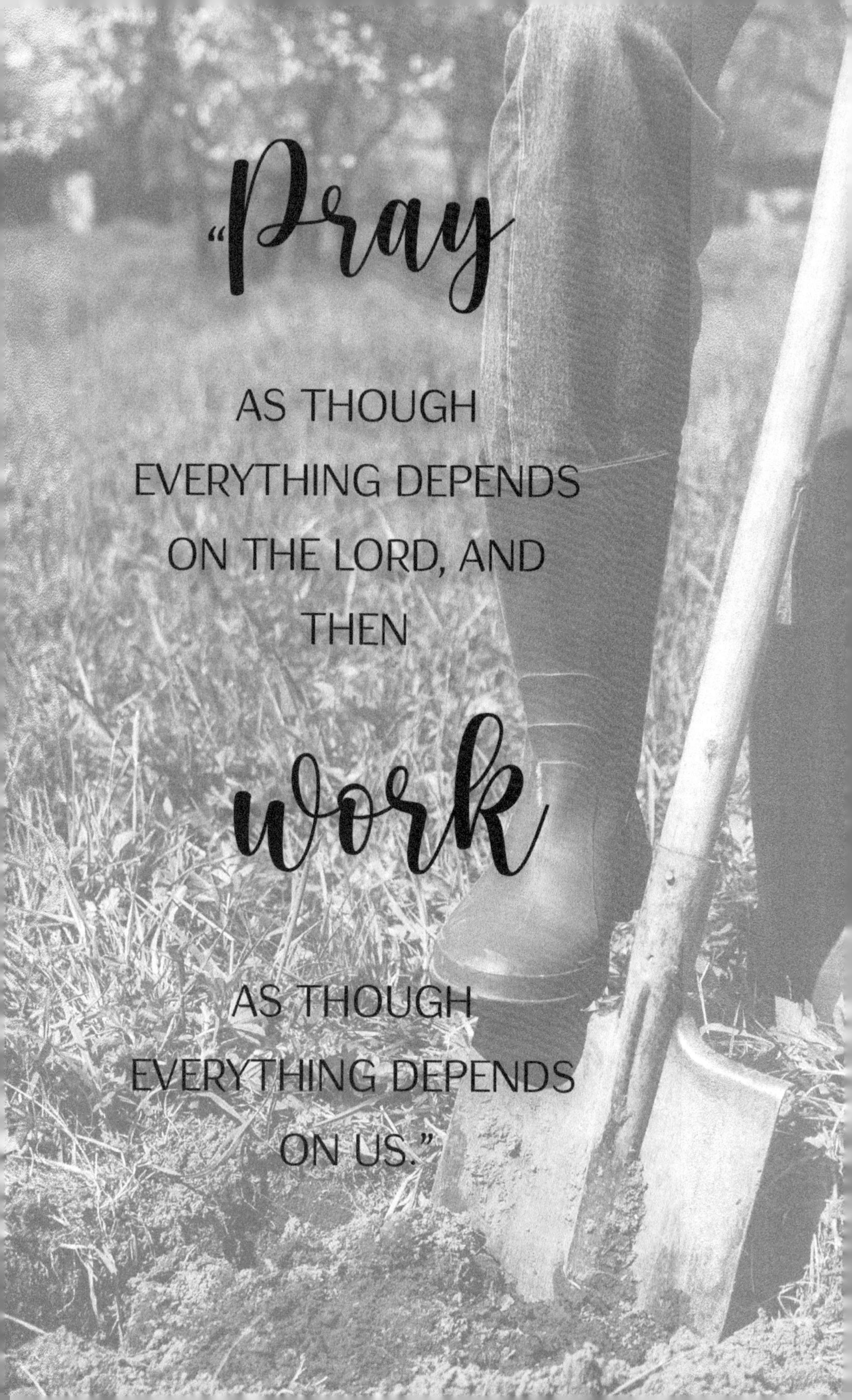
"Pray
AS THOUGH
EVERYTHING DEPENDS
ON THE LORD, AND
THEN
work
AS THOUGH
EVERYTHING DEPENDS
ON US."

righteous life, we will have the Holy Ghost poured down upon us. My faith is an integral part of who I am. As a disciple of Christ, my discipleship should infuse every aspect of my life. I strive to keep the armor of God molded to me. I view it more as Wolverine's adamantium rather than Iron Man's suit. It is not a bolt on and off accessory. Again, the way to do this is to live as disciples at all times, staying close to the Holy Ghost in our everyday lives through the things we do and the relationships we develop. In this way we are better prepared to hear Him among all of the competing voices that call to us.

I am not suggesting that we isolate ourselves from the world by digging deep moats or constructing barriers several meters high around our homes, but rather that in our family councils, under the influence of the Spirit, we establish the activities, entertainment, books, friendships, rules, and habits that will constitute our fortresses. Our fortress consists of teaching our children the gospel through the scriptures, establishing the habit of reading them every day as a family, and basing a large part of our conversations on them. It means kneeling together daily to pray and to teach our children the importance of direct, personal communication with our Heavenly Father (Horacio A. Tenorio, "Let Us Build Fortresses").

What defenses against the adversary
can I put into place in my own life?

What defenses against the adversary
can I put into place in my home?

Hearing Him requires effort

This opportunity to hear Him requires effort in our day-to-day living. His voice is not normally going to come unbidden or without us playing our part. One of my favorite maxims is "Pray as though everything depends on the Lord, and then work as though everything depends on us." We have to show to the Lord that our hearts are in the questions we are asking and that we truly want the enlightenment we are seeking. When translating the Book of Mormon, Oliver Cowdery petitioned the Lord for the opportunity to translate. This was granted to him, but then he failed. The Lord explained why this was the case:

> *Behold, you have not understood; you have supposed that I would give it unto you, when you took no thought save it was to ask me (D&C 9:7).*

While we may have the gift of the Holy Ghost, it is not automatic that we will receive and recognize revelation. In the example I shared earlier, I needed someone more conversant with the Spirit to help me understand when I was Hearing Him. By the same token, just because we ask does not mean we will automatically hear. Hearing Him requires us to put in some work; the Lord continues:

> *But, behold, I say unto you, that you must study it out in your mind; then you must ask me if it be right . . . (D&C 9:8).*

This work can come before or after the request (or both). Let me offer an example: I am married to Ruth. When I was younger, the Lord revealed to me that she was the woman I should marry and spend eternity with. I received this revelation after spending time with her, discussing all aspects of life and existence with her, and generally getting to know her. Having "studied it out in my mind," I went to the Lord and said, "I think Ruth is the one. Is she? I didn't go to a dance with the question, "Who should I marry?" and be told to pick Ruth from a room full of girls. That's not the way revelation works. We have an involvement in the process, and the Lord expects us to work with Him to Hear His voice. The same kind of example is shown in the story of the brother of Jared. The Lord could have told him to get the stones and He would light them, but He didn't. The process involved the brother of Jared being an active participant in the process.

Sometimes the voices that stop us from Hearing Him come from within us. They may include voices of doubt or voices of unworthiness. Perhaps we have listened to the flattering voices too much and have succumbed to the temptations of life that have drawn us away from the Holy Ghost and the opportunity to hear Him. By refocusing on the Savior and repenting, the glory of the Atonement of Jesus Christ is that it lifts us up. We might get lost in the mists of darkness for a period time, but the iron rod is where we left it. It will take our best efforts, the help of others, and the grace of Jesus Christ to find our way back, but the voices that tell us we are unworthy and shouldn't even try should be ignored.

We also hear Him more clearly as we refine our ability to recognize the whisperings of the Holy Ghost. It has never been more imperative to know how the Spirit speaks to you than right now. In the Godhead, the Holy Ghost is the messenger. He will bring thoughts to your mind which the Father and Son want you to receive. He is the Comforter. He will bring a feeling of peace to your heart. He testifies of truth and will confirm what is true as you hear and read the word of the Lord (Russell M. Nelson, "Hear Him").

How do I feel and hear the promptings of the Holy Ghost?

Hearing Him through the scriptures

One of the ways I can hear Him is in the scriptures. The scriptures are the prerecorded voice of the Lord. It is not hearing an audible voice per se, although that can happen. It is hearing the scriptures in a feeling—a feeling in my mind, a feeling in my heart. For me, the scriptures are key in receiving and recognizing those thoughts and feelings.

Even in a busy, fast-paced world, where many voices beckon for our attention, I can "be still," and "hear Him." As I strive to hear His voice in the scriptures, as I pray sincerely—not just saying prayers, but praying with a sincere heart and real intent—then according to the Lord's will and timing, I can be blessed in marvelous ways (David A. Bednar, "'Hear Him' in Your Heart and in Your Mind").

How can the iron rod, or the scriptures, help us hear Him? The scriptures were given under the inspiration of the Holy Ghost. When we study their words, we are able to Hear His voice. We cannot hope for new revelation if we fail to read and heed the recorded revelation that we have already received. President Henry B. Eyring outlined hearing the voice of the Lord through the scriptures:

> *He has used the scriptures to counsel me about my needs, my situation, and my life. But I learned that I must go to the scriptures in order to find that counsel ("How God Speaks to Me Through the Scriptures").*

We are able to feel of His love and hear His voice, but we are also able to recognize the dealings of the Lord with His people, and most especially with us. How is this possible through words? Let me share a personal experience that goes alongside this question. Before I met my wife I knew that I loved her. How? We had written to each other at least once a week for the last year of my mission. Through these letters I got to know all about Ruth, and she got to know all about me (with some very far away pictures thrown in). She probably got to know me better than most other people apart from my family. I often use this as an example of how a relationship can be developed through words. That is what the scriptures are able to do. Through studying them we are able to learn more about the Lord and feel more of His love and Hear His voice.

One of my early mentors in the Restored Gospel was Joseph Fielding McConkie. He was one of the greatest teachers I have had the pleasure to learn from. He, more than anyone I have ever served with, used the scriptures as the basis of all of his teaching. This taught me so much about Hearing the Lord. When he taught, he wasn't interested in what we learned from him but what we learned from the Lord. This has resonated with me throughout my life. When I was bishop and someone would come to me with an issue, I would invariably open the scriptures with them. This exercise served a number of purposes. First, it enabled us to seek the voice of the Lord within the scriptures and find an answer therein:

> *The scriptures are alive with characters and events that translate themselves into modern settings. Who has never, Enoch-like, at least felt like protesting a call to service with a "Why me?" attitude. "[I] am but a lad," Enoch argued, "[unpopular and] slow of speech" (Moses 6:31). Who has never experienced Jonah-like indignation when someone repents whom we did not expect to? (Jonah 4). Our own Church history is full of tyranny and villainy of Pharaohs, Herods, and Pilates; and is not the world still full of people who, Nicodemus-like, privately and quietly seek after the Church but publicly shun it?*

Are there no more doubting Thomases or impetuous Peters who dare rebuke the Lord? (Matt. 16:22). Or Amuleks who know the gospel is true but will not know it, who have heard the voice of the Lord but will not hear it? (Alma 10:5–6). Are there no more Professor Korihors who tell us that our religion consists of the "foolish traditions" of our fathers that we cannot know of things we cannot see, that all our religious belief is the result of a frenzied mind?
(Joseph Fielding McConkie, Teach and Reach, *14–15).*

We can find answers to our various circumstances through the scriptures. Second, the scriptures themselves open up the way to hear the Holy Ghost and the voice of the Lord. The Holy Ghost was the inspiration under which the scriptures were given. It makes perfect sense that as we read under that same Spirit we will be able to receive promptings and guidance and hear Him. The third purpose is to teach spiritual self-reliance. If I opened the scriptures as the first response to a query, it may be that next time the member would seek that revelation for themselves independent of seeking my guidance.

All of this highlights the well-used maxim: "If we want to speak to the Lord, we pray. If we want the Lord to speak to us, we read the scriptures." Even if the answer to our specific circumstance is not in the words of the scripture, the space that is opened up with the Holy Ghost as we read the words means that we can receive that answer through personal revelation.

I find that when I read the scriptures, I hear the Savior's voice and listen to the Spirit. I read what the Savior has said about Himself and about us. Things like "Seek ye first the kingdom of God and his righteousness, and all these things shall be added unto you." And "Come, follow me." And "If ye love me, keep my commandments." Those simple statements of the Savior remind me of what I want to be, where I want to be, and who I want to follow (Jean B. Bingham, "The More I 'Hear Him,' the More I Understand Him").

Scriptures I'm studying:

What have I learned from the scriptures about the Lord? About myself? Something I should do? Someone I should reach out to?

Hearing Him through prayer

Nephi teaches us that "*the evil spirit teacheth not a man to pray, but teacheth him that he must not pray*" (2 Nephi 32:8), which suggests that we should do all that we can to ignore that spirit and pray always. As with any attempt to hear Him, the most effective ways to learn of His will for us and His comfort in our lives is through scripture study and prayer.

Sometimes when we pray, we may not feel we receive answers. We may not Hear His voice. This will take time, but He is always there for us. As our prayers become earnest and we listen for answers, we will hear Him. Oliver Cowdery struggled with this. He had given up aspects of his career to come and help with the translation of the Book of Mormon. He worried that he had kind of fallen into this and that in so doing he had never felt the Holy Ghost confirming him in his path. On inquiring of the Lord through Joseph Smith, he received the following:

> *Verily, verily, I say unto you, if you desire a further witness, cast your mind upon the night that you cried unto me in your heart, that you might know concerning the truth of these things. Did I not speak peace to your mind concerning the matter? What greater witness can you have than from God? . . . Behold, thou art Oliver, and I have spoken unto thee because of thy desires; therefore treasure up these words in thy heart. Be faithful and diligent in keeping the commandments of God, and I will encircle thee in the arms of my love (D&C 6:20, 22–23).*

What a beautiful passage of scripture. The Lord confirms the answers to Oliver's prayers in a way that we can all hope for. He spoke peace to his mind. Surely this is what we are all seeking in our lives. Oliver is then promised the greatest blessing, one of comfort to us, that we can be encircled in the arms of the Savior's love. This isn't a promise for the celestial kingdom. This is a promise for the here and now. I can think of no closer expression of familial and friendly love than an embrace, and when we are in this embrace, we are so close as to be confidently able to hear Him.

> *There is a great lesson in that about muscular, urgent, determined prayer to fight through, whether it is the adversary's opposition, the cares of the day, or the distractions of our mind. We have many things that can keep us from having that divine experience. And we, like Joseph, will have to exert all our power to have the magnificent experience that God wants us to have. . . .*
>
> *The scriptures occasionally talk about the Lord speaking, and they sometimes describe His voice. Sometimes it is a soft voice. Sometimes it is a loud voice. But it is always a penetrating voice. It is always a voice that captivates and engages the whole soul. For me, to say out loud the words of my prayer is to make it crisp and almost visible. Prayer takes on a meaning and a life that is not quite the same when I am just thinking words or mumbling a bit. When we communicate clearly to Him, we can expect to "hear Him" more clearly in return (Jeffrey R. Holland, "To 'Hear Him' Is the Essence of the Restoration").*

How can I make my prayers stronger, more urgent and determined?

How can I make time to listen to the answers?

Hearing Him through the examples of others

One of my favorite hymns is "Each Life That Touches Ours for Good." Its words illustrate the influence of good people and friends in our lives.

Each life that touches ours for good
Reflects thine own great mercy, Lord.
Thou sendest blessings from above
Through words and deeds of those who love.

What greater gift dost thou bestow,
What greater goodness can we know
Than Christlike friends, whose gentle ways
Strengthen our faith, enrich our days.

When such a friend from us departs
We hold forever in our hearts
A sweet and hallowed memory,
Bringing us nearer, Lord, to thee.

For worthy friends whose lives proclaim
Devotion to the Savior's name,
Who bless our days with peace and love,
We praise thy goodness Lord above.

There are people who come into our lives, perhaps for a long time, perhaps only for a short season, but they come into our lives and touch our lives for good. Elder Jeffrey R. Holland describes some of these people as "angelic":

> *I have spoken here of heavenly help, of angels dispatched to bless us in time of need. But when we speak of those who are instruments in the hand of God, we are reminded that not all angels are from the other side of the veil. Some of them we walk with and talk with—here, now, every day. Some of them reside in our own neighborhoods. Some of them gave birth to us, and in my case, one of them consented to marry me. Indeed heaven never seems closer than when we see the love of God manifested in the kindness and devotion of people so good and so pure that angelic is the only word that comes to mind ("The Ministry of Angels").*

I wrote earlier about the influence of my wife, Ruth, on my striving to be more like Christ. There have been many others throughout my life who have helped me become better and more Christlike. As I think of others, I think of my mum and certain teachers. My mum is amazing! At age 23 she was left a widow with two young sons to care for and look after. She had O levels and not many other qualifications since she hadn't been allowed to stay in school because of needing to earn money. As a child, I didn't know that we lived in difficult circumstances or that life had dealt my mum a harsh set of cards. I knew I was loved. I also knew of the value of hard work since my mum worked in a series of jobs that enabled her to be there for us, including working as a barmaid and a care assistant. I was also taught that I could achieve anything I wanted to—the sky was the limit—or at least that is what my mum taught me. I often tell a story that I have never had the opportunity to test. Apparently, if you put mosquitoes in a jar with no lid, they jump out. I think that's fairly obvious. If you put them in a jar with a lid, they still try to jump out but are prevented from doing so by the lid. Again, no real surprise. However, if you take the lid off at that point, the mosquitoes only jump as high as the level of the lid because they have been taught that they can't go any higher. There was no lid placed on my imagination or ambition.

A few years ago, I was asked to be on a Q&A panel for a Young Single Adult fireside. One of the questions asked was whether you should always say yes when asked on a date. My daughter was also on a panel and gave her opinion as a YSA after I said no. She disagreed with me and said she liked to think of a date not as a marriage proposal, but as the opportunity to get to know someone and learn something from him. I liked that answer. Why have we been placed in a situation? Elder Ronald Rasband suggested that "Our lives are like a chessboard, and the Lord moves us from one place to another—if we are responsive to spiritual promptings. Looking back, we can see His hand in our lives" ("By Divine Design"). We are where we are because of the influence we can have. In recognizing this, Elder Rasband quoted Elder Neal A. Maxwell:

> *None of us ever fully utilizes the people-opportunities allocated to us within our circles of friendship. You and I may call these intersectings "coincidence." This word is understandable for mortals to use, but coincidence is not an appropriate word to describe the workings of an omniscient God. He does not do things by "coincidence" but . . . by "divine design" ("By Divine Design").*

Returning to Elder Holland's "angelic beings," we must ask questions about why we're placed in certain circumstances and with certain people. Many times we learn a lot by our interaction with others. We can hear the promptings of the Lord to rise up and be better. Sometimes that is in emulating other Christlike people. Sometimes that is by us being called to Christlike service. We hear Him through being friends with those who enable us to be our best selves.

> *Since my youth I have sought to "hear Him." One of the ways I heard the Lord in my youth was through my wife. We were childhood sweethearts and dated in high school—she had a tremendous impact on me (Jeffrey R. Holland, "To 'Hear Him' Is the Essence of the Restoration").*

Who are the people who have an impact on me in drawing close to the Lord and Hearing Him?

How can I help others hear Him through my actions?

Up to this point, I have spoken about those we know well, but it is not limited to just our friends. In fact, Christlike service is often tested the most with people we don't know. We often hear the call to be "His hands," to stand in His place, and do the things the Savior would do if He were here. In fulfilling the second great commandment to "love thy neighbor as thyself" (Matthew 22:36), we open ourselves up to the Spirit and Hearing Him as we stand in His place. In one of my favorite stories, "Where Love Is, God Is," Tolstoy tells of a cobbler named Martin. After a life of hardship and striving to live a good life, he wondered about his standing before God. He heard the Lord's voice telling him that if he looked into the street the next day, the Lord would visit him. Martin arose early the next morning and made a fire. He tidied his room and sat down at the window. He saw three people:

The first was an old man struggling with the backbreaking work of clearing the snow. Martin had compassion and invited him in for a warm drink while he waited for the Savior.
The second was a woman with her baby. She was poorly dressed for the winter weather, and both she and the baby looked tired and cold. In her threadbare clothes, she struggled to soothe the baby. Martin called to her and invited her to come in and warm by the fire. He gave her some of the bread and cabbage soup he had prepared and looked after the baby while she ate. Before she left, he gave her some clothes and his cloak.
The third was a young boy who was being roughly treated by a woman he had just stolen an apple from. Martin paid the woman for the apple, and the boy left carrying the woman's bag for her.

That night he shut up his shop and was ruing his overactive imagination when he heard the same voice calling him, saying, "Inasmuch as ye have done it unto one of the least of these . . . ye have done it unto me" (Matthew 25:40). The original story has so much more detail, but for the purpose of this book, this shortened version illustrates the opportunity we have to hear and experience the Savior in our lives. His Spirit is available to all of us as we strive to serve others.

A passage from the novel Les Misérables illustrates how priesthood holders can treat those individuals viewed as strangers. Jean Valjean had just been released as a prisoner. Exhausted by a long voyage and dying of hunger and thirst, he arrives in a small town seeking a place to find food and shelter for the night. When the news of his arrival spreads, one by one all the inhabitants close their doors to him. Not the hotel, not the inn, not even the prison would invite him in. He is rejected, driven away, banished. Finally, with no strength left, he collapses at the front door of the town's bishop.

The good clergyman is entirely aware of Valjean's background, but he invites the vagabond into his home with these compassionate words:

"'This is not my house; it is the house of Jesus Christ. This door does not demand of him who enters whether he has a name, but whether he has a grief. You suffer, you are hungry and thirsty; you are welcome. . . . What need have I to know your name? Besides, before you told me [your name], you had one which I knew.'

"[Valjean] opened his eyes in astonishment.

"'Really? You knew what I was called?'

"'Yes,' replied the Bishop. 'You are called my brother'" (Gerald Causse, "Ye Are No More Strangers").

What experiences have I had when I have seen the Savior's love in action?

How can I be more aware of the opportunities to hear Him through loving others?

Hearing Him through the words of the Prophets

What I the Lord have spoken, I have spoken, and I excuse not myself; and though the heavens and the earth pass away, my word shall not pass away, but shall all be fulfilled, whether by mine own voice or by the voice of my servants, it is the same (D&C 1:38).

As a new member of the Church beginning my first year of seminary, this was the first scripture I learned. It has remained with me ever since, and I often reflect on it as I prepare for general conference and as I read the words of the prophets and apostles. It is key for me to know that when I listen to the words of the prophets, I am putting myself in a position to hear the voice of the Lord. I remember once listening to general conference and questioning the relevance of what I was hearing to my life. President Gordon B. Hinckley was sharing a message about gambling and how we should guard against it. I thought, "What does this have to do with me? This must be an issue in the USA." Six months later, as I watched the rise of online gambling and the numerous television adverts and sport sponsorships from betting companies, I was grateful for the foresight of a living prophet.

We are promised in the scriptures that there are blessings associated with hearkening to the voice of the prophets:

Wherefore, meaning the church, thou shalt give heed unto all his words and commandments which he shall give unto you as he receiveth them, walking in all holiness before me; For his word ye shall receive, as if from mine own mouth, in all patience and faith. For by doing these things the gates of hell shall not prevail against you; yea, and the Lord God will disperse the powers of darkness from before you, and cause the heavens to shake for your good, and his name's glory (D&C 21:4–6).

As we hearken to the prophet, we are able to hear the Lord, and we are promised increased strength against the temptations that assail us. For me, hearken is to listen and do.

The very first word in the Doctrine and Covenants is hearken. It means "to listen with the intent to obey." To hearken means to "hear Him"—to hear what the Savior says and then to heed His counsel. In those two words—"Hear Him"—God gives us the pattern for success, happiness, and joy in this life. We are to hear the words of the Lord, hearken to them, and heed what He has told us!
(Russell M. Nelson, "Hear Him")

As we immerse ourselves in the words of the prophets, they help us draw closer to the Savior and be able to recognize and hear His voice in every aspect of our lives.

A few years ago, I was called to assist in the preparation and writing of *Teachings of the Presidents of the Church: Gordon B. Hinckley*. My first task was to read every talk President Hinckley had ever given as an Assistant to the Twelve, a member of the Quorum of the Twelve Apostles, a member of the First Presidency, and then as President of the Church (with emphasis on those he had delivered as President of the Church). Those two weeks are among some of the most memorable of my Church service. I felt a connection with President Hinckley. As I read, I was able to hear his distinctive voice speaking some of the words. But the greatest blessing was that I was able to see the Lord at work in his life and words, and I was able to draw closer to Him through that intensive reading.

This isn't a realistic proposition for many of us in such a short period of time, but there are other things we can do. The first thing we can do is to take notes as we listen to or study the words from general conference. As I take notes, I often include a verbatim quote I have just heard from the speaker that I feel I should remember and return to at a later point. Scattered through my notes are bracketed jottings that are preceded by the acronym PN (personal note). In these notes I record any impressions I might have while listening to the words of the talk. These might include prompts to action or thoughts about what I'm learning at that particular moment. As much as I am inspired by the exact words I hear, I am equally inspired by being open to the Holy Ghost in hearing what He has for me personally.

The second thing I might suggest is a habit I acquired a number of years ago. For those of you old enough to remember "Teachings of our Time," the fourth Sunday lesson for priesthood and Relief Society, I was responsible in my stake for the selection of topics. By the Tuesday after conference I was receiving messages from members of the stake asking what the topics were. I wasn't that quick, but in the week following conference, I listened to the entire general conference again as I drove to work. This intensive listening enabled me to see themes that emerged and helped me set goals and actions based on what I had learned.

Allowing the words of the prophets and apostles to infuse our lives and study really does help us live a more Christlike life. Talks or quotes will stand out to us as we try to live a more consecrated life as a disciple of Jesus Christ.

We are to seek, in every way we can, to hear Jesus Christ, who speaks to us through the power and ministering of the Holy Ghost. The purpose of this and every general conference is to help us hear Him. We have prayed and invite you to pray that the Spirit of the Lord will be with us in such rich abundance that you can hear the messages that the Savior has especially for you—messages that will bring peace to your soul. Messages that will heal your broken heart. Messages that will illuminate your mind. Messages that will help you know what to do as you move ahead through times of turmoil and trial (Russell M. Nelson, "Opening Message").

How can I prepare before general conference to hear the Spirit?

Speaker:

What was the topic?

What doctrine is being taught?

Scriptures that resonated with me during the talk:

Inspiration I received while listening to this talk:

Favorite thing this speaker said:

Themes I saw in the talk:

How did the Spirit touch my heart in this talk?

Speaker: ______________________

What was the topic? ______________________

____

What doctrine is being taught? ______________________

____

____

____

Scriptures that resonated with me during the talk: ______________________

____

____

____

Inspiration I received while listening to this talk: ______________________

____

____

____

Favorite thing this speaker said: ______________________

____

____

____

Themes I saw in the talk: ______________________

____

____

____

How did the Spirit touch my heart in this talk? ______________________

____

____

____

Speaker: ______________________________

What was the topic? ______________________________

____

What doctrine is being taught? ______________________________

____

____

____

Scriptures that resonated with me during the talk: ______________________________

____

____

____

Inspiration I received while listening to this talk: ______________________________

____

____

____

Favorite thing this speaker said: ______________________________

____

____

____

Themes I saw in the talk: ______________________________

____

____

____

How did the Spirit touch my heart in this talk? ______________________________

____

____

____

Speaker: ______________________________

What was the topic? ______________________________

____

What doctrine is being taught? ______________________________

____

____

____

Scriptures that resonated with me during the talk: ______________________________

____

____

____

Inspiration I received while listening to this talk: ______________________________

____

____

____

Favorite thing this speaker said: ______________________________

____

____

____

Themes I saw in the talk: ______________________________

____

____

____

How did the Spirit touch my heart in this talk? ______________________________

____

____

____

Speaker: ____________________

What was the topic? ____________________

What doctrine is being taught? ____________________

Scriptures that resonated with me during the talk: ____________________

Inspiration I received while listening to this talk: ____________________

Favorite thing this speaker said: ____________________

Themes I saw in the talk: ____________________

How did the Spirit touch my heart in this talk? ____________________

Speaker: ______________________________

What was the topic? ______________________________

____

What doctrine is being taught? ______________________________

____

____

____

Scriptures that resonated with me during the talk: ______________________________

____

____

____

Inspiration I received while listening to this talk: ______________________________

____

____

____

Favorite thing this speaker said: ______________________________

____

____

____

Themes I saw in the talk: ______________________________

____

____

____

How did the Spirit touch my heart in this talk? ______________________________

____

____

____

Speaker: ____________________

What was the topic? ____________________

What doctrine is being taught? ____________________

Scriptures that resonated with me during the talk: ____________________

Inspiration I received while listening to this talk: ____________________

Favorite thing this speaker said: ____________________

Themes I saw in the talk: ____________________

How did the Spirit touch my heart in this talk? ____________________

Speaker: ______________________________

What was the topic? ______________________________

____

What doctrine is being taught? ______________________________

____

____

____

Scriptures that resonated with me during the talk: ______________________________

____

____

____

Inspiration I received while listening to this talk: ______________________________

____

____

____

Favorite thing this speaker said: ______________________________

____

____

____

Themes I saw in the talk: ______________________________

____

____

____

How did the Spirit touch my heart in this talk? ______________________________

____

____

____

Speaker: ___

What was the topic? ___

What doctrine is being taught? ___

Scriptures that resonated with me during the talk: ___

Inspiration I received while listening to this talk: ___

Favorite thing this speaker said: ___

Themes I saw in the talk: ___

How did the Spirit touch my heart in this talk? ___

Speaker: ____________________

What was the topic? ____________________

____

What doctrine is being taught? ____________________

____

____

____

Scriptures that resonated with me during the talk: ____________________

____

____

____

Inspiration I received while listening to this talk: ____________________

____

____

____

Favorite thing this speaker said: ____________________

____

____

____

Themes I saw in the talk: ____________________

____

____

____

How did the Spirit touch my heart in this talk? ____________________

____

____

____

Speaker: ____________________

What was the topic? ____________________

What doctrine is being taught? ____________________

Scriptures that resonated with me during the talk: ____________________

Inspiration I received while listening to this talk: ____________________

Favorite thing this speaker said: ____________________

Themes I saw in the talk: ____________________

How did the Spirit touch my heart in this talk? ____________________

Speaker: ______________________________

What was the topic? ______________________________

____

What doctrine is being taught? ______________________________

____

____

____

Scriptures that resonated with me during the talk: ______________________________

____

____

____

Inspiration I received while listening to this talk: ______________________________

____

____

____

Favorite thing this speaker said: ______________________________

____

____

____

Themes I saw in the talk: ______________________________

____

____

____

How did the Spirit touch my heart in this talk? ______________________________

____

____

____

Speaker: ______________________________

What was the topic? ______________________________

____

What doctrine is being taught? ______________________________

____

____

____

Scriptures that resonated with me during the talk: ______________________________

____

____

____

Inspiration I received while listening to this talk: ______________________________

____

____

____

Favorite thing this speaker said: ______________________________

____

____

____

Themes I saw in the talk: ______________________________

____

____

____

How did the Spirit touch my heart in this talk? ______________________________

____

____

____

Speaker: ______________________________

What was the topic? ______________________________

____

What doctrine is being taught? ______________________________

____

____

____

Scriptures that resonated with me during the talk: ______________________________

____

____

____

Inspiration I received while listening to this talk: ______________________________

____

____

____

Favorite thing this speaker said: ______________________________

____

____

____

Themes I saw in the talk: ______________________________

____

____

____

How did the Spirit touch my heart in this talk? ______________________________

____

____

____

Speaker: ____________________

What was the topic? ____________________

____

What doctrine is being taught? ____________________

____

____

____

Scriptures that resonated with me during the talk: ____________________

____

____

____

Inspiration I received while listening to this talk: ____________________

____

____

____

Favorite thing this speaker said: ____________________

____

____

____

Themes I saw in the talk: ____________________

____

____

____

How did the Spirit touch my heart in this talk? ____________________

____

____

____

Speaker:

What was the topic?

What doctrine is being taught?

Scriptures that resonated with me during the talk:

Inspiration I received while listening to this talk:

Favorite thing this speaker said:

Themes I saw in the talk:

How did the Spirit touch my heart in this talk?

Speaker: ___

What was the topic? ___

___

What doctrine is being taught? ___

___

___

___

Scriptures that resonated with me during the talk: ___

___

___

___

Inspiration I received while listening to this talk: ___

___

___

___

Favorite thing this speaker said: ___

___

___

___

Themes I saw in the talk: ___

___

___

___

How did the Spirit touch my heart in this talk? ___

___

___

___

Speaker:

What was the topic?

What doctrine is being taught?

Scriptures that resonated with me during the talk:

Inspiration I received while listening to this talk:

Favorite thing this speaker said:

Themes I saw in the talk:

How did the Spirit touch my heart in this talk?

Speaker:

What was the topic?

What doctrine is being taught?

Scriptures that resonated with me during the talk:

Inspiration I received while listening to this talk:

Favorite thing this speaker said:

Themes I saw in the talk:

How did the Spirit touch my heart in this talk?

Speaker: ______________________________

What was the topic? ______________________________

____

What doctrine is being taught? ______________________________

____

____

____

Scriptures that resonated with me during the talk: ______________________________

____

____

____

Inspiration I received while listening to this talk: ______________________________

____

____

____

Favorite thing this speaker said: ______________________________

____

____

____

Themes I saw in the talk: ______________________________

____

____

____

How did the Spirit touch my heart in this talk? ______________________________

____

____

____

Speaker: ______________________________

What was the topic? ______________________________

____

What doctrine is being taught? ______________________________

____

____

____

Scriptures that resonated with me during the talk: ______________________________

____

____

____

Inspiration I received while listening to this talk: ______________________________

____

____

____

Favorite thing this speaker said: ______________________________

____

____

____

Themes I saw in the talk: ______________________________

____

____

____

How did the Spirit touch my heart in this talk? ______________________________

____

____

____

Speaker: ____________________

What was the topic? ____________________

____

What doctrine is being taught? ____________________

____

____

____

Scriptures that resonated with me during the talk: ____________________

____

____

____

Inspiration I received while listening to this talk: ____________________

____

____

____

Favorite thing this speaker said: ____________________

____

____

____

Themes I saw in the talk: ____________________

____

____

____

How did the Spirit touch my heart in this talk? ____________________

____

____

____

Speaker: ______________________________

What was the topic? ______________________________

____

What doctrine is being taught? ______________________________

____

____

____

Scriptures that resonated with me during the talk: ______________________________

____

____

____

Inspiration I received while listening to this talk: ______________________________

____

____

____

Favorite thing this speaker said: ______________________________

____

____

____

Themes I saw in the talk: ______________________________

____

____

____

How did the Spirit touch my heart in this talk? ______________________________

____

____

____

Speaker: ______________________________

What was the topic? ______________________________

____

What doctrine is being taught? ______________________________

____

____

____

Scriptures that resonated with me during the talk: ______________________________

____

____

____

Inspiration I received while listening to this talk: ______________________________

____

____

____

Favorite thing this speaker said: ______________________________

____

____

____

Themes I saw in the talk: ______________________________

____

____

____

How did the Spirit touch my heart in this talk? ______________________________

____

____

____

Speaker: ________________________________

What was the topic? ________________________________

____

What doctrine is being taught? ________________________________

____

____

____

Scriptures that resonated with me during the talk: ________________

____

____

____

Inspiration I received while listening to this talk: ________________

____

____

____

Favorite thing this speaker said: ________________________

____

____

____

Themes I saw in the talk: ________________________________

____

____

____

How did the Spirit touch my heart in this talk? ________________

____

____

____

Speaker:

What was the topic?

What doctrine is being taught?

Scriptures that resonated with me during the talk:

Inspiration I received while listening to this talk:

Favorite thing this speaker said:

Themes I saw in the talk:

How did the Spirit touch my heart in this talk?

Speaker:

What was the topic?

What doctrine is being taught?

Scriptures that resonated with me during the talk:

Inspiration I received while listening to this talk:

Favorite thing this speaker said:

Themes I saw in the talk:

How did the Spirit touch my heart in this talk?

Speaker:

What was the topic?

What doctrine is being taught?

Scriptures that resonated with me during the talk:

Inspiration I received while listening to this talk:

Favorite thing this speaker said:

Themes I saw in the talk:

How did the Spirit touch my heart in this talk?

Speaker: ______________________________

What was the topic? ______________________________

____

What doctrine is being taught? ______________________________

____

____

____

Scriptures that resonated with me during the talk: ______________________________

____

____

____

Inspiration I received while listening to this talk: ______________________________

____

____

____

Favorite thing this speaker said: ______________________________

____

____

____

Themes I saw in the talk: ______________________________

____

____

____

How did the Spirit touch my heart in this talk? ______________________________

____

____

____

Speaker: ______________________________

What was the topic? ______________________________

____

What doctrine is being taught? ______________________________

____

____

____

Scriptures that resonated with me during the talk: ______________________________

____

____

____

Inspiration I received while listening to this talk: ______________________________

____

____

____

Favorite thing this speaker said: ______________________________

____

____

____

Themes I saw in the talk: ______________________________

____

____

____

How did the Spirit touch my heart in this talk? ______________________________

____

____

____

Speaker:

What was the topic?

What doctrine is being taught?

Scriptures that resonated with me during the talk:

Inspiration I received while listening to this talk:

Favorite thing this speaker said:

Themes I saw in the talk:

How did the Spirit touch my heart in this talk?

In closing

What will happen as you more intentionally hear, hearken, and heed what the Savior has said and what He is saying now through His prophets? I promise that you will be blessed with additional power to deal with temptation, struggles, and weaknesses. I promise miracles in your marriage, family relationships, and daily work. And I promise that your capacity to feel joy will increase even if turbulence increases in your life (Russell M. Nelson, "Hear Him").

We live in a noisy and chaotic world. We live in the time that Amos saw—a time of famine in Hearing the Lord. As members of The Church of Jesus Christ of Latter-day Saints, we are not immune from this famine, but we do have the knowledge to know how to find the nourishment that comes from Hearing Him. We know that as we build on the rock of our Savior and the rock of revelation we will be able stand:

> *. . . that when the devil shall send forth his mighty winds, yea, his shafts in the whirlwind, yea, when all his hail and his mighty storm shall beat upon you, it shall have no power over you to drag you down to the gulf of misery and endless wo, because of the rock upon which ye are built, which is a sure foundation, a foundation whereon if men build they cannot fall (Helaman 5:12).*

In our busy lives we need to find time for Him. We need to "be still" and seek His Hands in our lives. It is impossible unless we actively seek Him. There are so many competing voices vying for our attention that we need to become conversant in the language of the Spirit so we can understand His will for each of us personally. The answer is sincere commitment to a meaningful, personal, and private devotion to a life of revelation and ongoing sanctification. We can consider carefully those actions that will fill our lives with the Holy Ghost and the ability to Hear Him. All our actions are outward expressions of our faith in the Lord Jesus Christ and our desire to Hear Him in our lives. As we Hear Him, we recognize the importance of gospel living so we will seek to Hear Him in every aspect of our lives and allow Him to calm the storms of mortality.

References

Neil L. Andersen (2020) Spiritually Defining Memories available at https://www.churchofjesuschrist.org/study/general-conference/2020/04/15andersen?lang=eng

David A. Bednar (2016) Always Retain a Remission of Your Sins available at https://www.churchofjesuschrist.org/study/general-conference/2016/04/always-retain-a-remission-of-your-sins?lang=eng

David A. Bednar (2020) "Hear Him" in Your Heart and in Your Mind available athttps://www.churchofjesuschrist.org/inspiration/hear-him-in-your-heart-and-in-your-mind?lang=eng

Jean B. Bingham (2020) The More I "Hear Him," the More I Understand Him available at https://www.churchofjesuschrist.org/inspiration/the-more-i-hear-him-the-more-i-understand-him?lang=eng

Gerald Causse (2013) Ye Are No More Strangers available at https://www.churchofjesuschrist.org/study/general-conference/2013/10/ye-are-no-more-strangers?lang=eng

D. Todd Christofferson (2008) Born Again available at https://www.churchofjesuschrist.org/study/general-conference/2008/04/born-again?lang=eng

Michelle D. Craig (2019) Spiritual Capacity available at https://www.churchofjesuschrist.org/study/general-conference/2019/10/15craig?lang=ase

Michelle D. Craig (2020) Eyes to See available at https://www.churchofjesuschrist.org/study/general-conference/2020/10/14craig?lang=eng

Henry B. Eyring (2019) How God Speaks to Me Through the Scriptures available at https://www.churchofjesuschrist.org/inspiration/how-god-speaks-to-me-through-the-scriptures?lang=eng

James E. Faust (2001) Stories From My Life, Salt Lake City: Deseret Book
Jeffrey R. Holland (2006) Broken Things to Mend available at https://www.churchofjesuschrist.org/study/general-conference/2006/04/broken-things-to-mend?lang=eng

Jeffrey R. Holland (2008) The Ministry of Angels available at https://www.churchofjesuschrist.org/study/general-conference/2008/10/the-ministry-of-angels?lang=eng

Jeffrey R. Holland (2020) To "Hear Him" Is the Essence of the Restoration available at https://www.churchofjesuschrist.org/inspiration/to-hear-him-is-the-essence-of-the-restoration?lang=eng

David P. Homer (2019) Hearing His Voice available at https://www.churchofjesuschrist.org/study/general-conference/2019/04/27homer?lang=eng

Russell M. Nelson (2020) Opening Message available at https://www.churchofjesuschrist.org/study/general-conference/2020/04/11nelson?lang=eng

Russell M. Nelson (2020) Hear Him available at https://www.churchofjesuschrist.org/study/general-conference/2020/04/45nelson?lang=eng

David O. McKay, (1953) Gospel Ideals compiled by G. Homer Durham. Salt Lake City: The Improvement Era

Parley P. Pratt (1978). [1855]. Key to the Science of Theology. Salt Lake City: Deseret Book.

Joseph Fielding Smith (1971) Take Heed to Yourselves, compiled by Joseph Fielding Smith, Jr., Salt Lake City: Deseret Book

Ronald A. Rasband (2017) By Divine Design available at https://www.churchofjesuschrist.org/study/general-conference/2017/10/by-divine-design?lang=eng

Horacio A. Tenorio (1994) Let Us Build Fortresses available at https://www.churchofjesuschrist.org/study/general-conference/1994/10/let-us-build-fortresses?lang=eng